IT'S TIME TO EAT UGLI FRUIT

It's Time to Eat UGLI FRUIT

Walter the Educator

Silent King Books
A WhichHead Entertainment Imprint

Copyright © 2025 by Walter the Educator

All rights reserved. No part of this book may be reproduced in any manner whatsoever without written per- mission except in the case of brief quotations embodied in critical articles and reviews.

First Printing, 2024

Disclaimer

This book is a literary work; the story is not about specific persons, locations, situations, and/or circumstances unless mentioned in a historical context. Any resemblance to real persons, locations, situations, and/or circumstances is coincidental. This book is for entertainment and informational purposes only. The author and publisher offer this information without warranties expressed or implied. No matter the grounds, neither the author nor the publisher will be accountable for any losses, injuries, or other damages caused by the reader's use of this book. The use of this book acknowledges an understanding and acceptance of this disclaimer.

It's Time to Eat UGLI FRUIT is a collectible early learning book by Walter the Educator suitable for all ages belonging to Walter the Educator's Time to Eat Book Series. Collect more books at WaltertheEducator.com

USE THE EXTRA SPACE TO TAKE NOTES AND DOCUMENT YOUR MEMORIES

UGLI FRUIT

It's time to eat Ugli fruit, oh wow!

It's Time to Eat Ugli fruit

A funny name, but let's learn how.

It's bumpy and big, not smooth like some,

But inside it's sweet, come get you some!

Its color is orange, yellow, or green,

The coolest fruit you've ever seen.

Peel it back, and there you'll find,

Juicy goodness of the citrus kind.

The taste is tangy, sweet, and bright,

A fruity snack that feels just right.

Like a mix of orange and grapefruit too,

Ugli fruit's flavor will amaze you!

It grows in trees, so tall and strong,

In sunny places where it belongs.

The farmers pick it when it's ripe,

To share this fruit of every stripe.

It's Time to Eat
Ugli fruit

Packed with vitamins, so good for you,

It helps your body stay healthy too.

A boost of energy, a happy bite,

Ugli fruit keeps you feeling just right!

You can eat it plain or squeeze the juice,

For breakfast drinks, it's got great use.

In salads or snacks, it's always a win,

A treat that brings a big smile in!

Though its name is Ugli, don't you fret,

It's Time to Eat Ugli fruit

It's one of the best fruits you've tasted yet.

It teaches us all, don't judge by a look,

What's on the inside is what we should book!

The bees and the sunshine help it grow,

With nature's magic, as we all know.

From flowers to fruit, it's quite a sight,

Ugli fruit makes everything bright!

Let's share it with friends and pass it around,

This special fruit that we've all found.

A snack so cheerful, a fun little prize,

The joy of Ugli fruit never dies!

It's Time to Eat
Ugli fruit

So next time you see this fruit so rare,

Pick it up and show you care.

It's time to eat Ugli fruit, let's cheer,

A funny name, but a fruit so dear!

ABOUT THE CREATOR

Walter the Educator is one of the pseudonyms for Walter Anderson. Formally educated in Chemistry, Business, and Education, he is an educator, an author, a diverse entrepreneur, and he is the son of a disabled war veteran. "Walter the Educator" shares his time between educating and creating. He holds interests and owns several creative projects that entertain, enlighten, enhance, and educate, hoping to inspire and motivate you. Follow, find new works, and stay up to date with Walter the Educator™

at WaltertheEducator.com

www.ingramcontent.com/pod-product-compliance
Lightning Source LLC
LaVergne TN
LVHW05201606052
838201LV00059B/4048